# don't try

### nathan brown

&

### jon dee graham

MEZCALITA PRESS, LLC
Norman, Oklahoma

first edition, 2016
copyright © 2016 by nathan brown
                              & jon dee graham
all rights reserved
ISBN-13: 978-0-9837383-7-4

library of congress control number: 2016910707

editorial assistance: Ashley Brown
cover design: Jen Rickard Blair
cover photography: Rodney Bursiel
internal photography: Rodney Bursiel


MEZCALITA PRESS, LLC
Norman, Oklahoma

don't try

books by nathan brown

*My Salvaged Heart: Story of a Cautious Courtship*
*To Sing Hallucinated: First Thoughts on Last Words*
*Oklahoma Poems… and Their Poets*
*Less Is More, More or Less*
*Karma Crisis: New and Selected Poems*
*Letters to the One-Armed Poet*
*My Sideways Heart*
*Two Tables Over*
*Not Exactly Job*
*Suffer the Little Voices*
*Ashes Over the Southwest*
*Hobson's Choice*

CDs by nathan brown

*Driftin' Away*
*The Why in the Road*
*Gypsy Moon*

books and CDs by jon dee graham

graham has released ten albums as a
solo artist and (according to
AllMusicGuide) has contributed
songs/performance/production to over
sixty albums since 1980.

Wisconsin Brewing Company has named
three different beers after his lyrics
and songs, and he recently released a
collection of illustrated notes to his
wife, titled 'LOVE, noted from The
Bear' available on Amazon and
www.jondeegraham.com

# table of contents

# acknowledge ments

nathan sends thanks to Lise Liddell for so much "brave believing," Kellie Salome, Rodney Bursiel, and to the *Southern Literary Review* for his worst-ever review... as well as to Bukowski, who always pulled his head back out from academia's ivory ass. but also, and always, to Ashley Brown, Norma and Lavonn Brown, and Sierra Brown.

jon dee sends thanks to Gretchen and William and Roy, and *NME Magazine* for his worst-ever review... as well as to Buk and his typer for making the tough times bearable... the hard clear line has never failed me.

we both thank Ashley Brown for her editing skills and catching mistakes that would have embarrassed us both.

thanks to the *Switchgrass Review* for first publishing "men often crawl."

thanks to *Conclave, Fall 2016, Vol. 10* for first publishing "I think of guitars under the sea," "22 cans of Campbell's soup," and "every time my toilet flushes."

and thanks to *Red Truck Review – Issue 5* for first publishing "zero times zero times zero" and "dying for and of life."

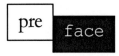

the title of each poem in this book is a line or phrase taken from Charles Bukowski's poetry. plain and simple. if we get sued, we get sued. but we *did* give him credit. and while we don't think the old bastard would care, who knows what his publisher will think...

we both love the guy. and even though he wrote way too many horse racing poems, we wanted to honor him somehow...

hell, even the title of the book comes straight from Bukowski's gravestone...

Woke up this morning and it seemed to me
that every night turns out to be
a little bit more like Bukowski

~ Modest Mouse
"Bukowski"

# don't try

# nathan brown

## &

### jon dee graham

"bukowski bear"

~ jon dee graham

## zero times zero times zero

an accountant calculating
a poet's taxes late at night
on April the Fourteenth.

the distance between my beliefs
and my illusions
divided by what I know.

the nightmares of traders
when Wall Street sleeps.

the barometric pressure
in this room when I'm done.

the miles per hour
at the end of the accident.

my current credibility rating.

the sum-total of my sadness,
or concern, when this year's
election cycle is finally over.

I think of guitars under the sea

and the musicians
who try to play them,
floating along and around
in the wake of a shark's tail fin.


I think of Little John Thunders
digging in his boot
for that last balloon
lest it get wet
and the dreams wash away,

and of Monet's unwashed brushes
as they sank on down to the bottom
of the River Epte, the paint still wet,

the eyes of the turtles and minnows
fascinated by the impression they left
in violet trails on the way down.


I think of mopey Jimmy Morrison
pushing all those terrified horses
off the deck and into the ocean
and then trying—unsuccessfully—
to ride them through the fear
and salted foam,

and of all the troubles
Shakespeare would've had
if Hamlet had been a happier,
more well-adjusted young man.

so when you look at the thing,
and I mean really look at it,
it's hard NOT to think
of guitars under the sea.

# the laughter of the hidden gods

sure,
I didn't know
what it was back then,
but I'm certain I'd heard it
as early as the 4<sup>th</sup> or 5<sup>th</sup> grade.

what else could explain
that friend in homeroom
who used to etch and scrape
emotional milestones into her forearms
with scissors she stole from art class
because her parents were busy
plotting each other's murder?

or, say, Charlie Manson's
strange love for messy
installation pieces?

so it helped me, later on,
when Bukowski finally
barged into the bushes,
pulled their hidden boxers
down around their godly ankles,
and then paraded them out
for me to see.

when you get a good look at them
it's sorta sad how small and homely
are the hidden gods...

less like gods and
more like garden-gnomes.

a queer compassion for them
arises in me
and I think: wow
if that were me
I suppose I'd hide too...

crouching
hidden in the hedge,
supine in the sandbox,
fast behind the trashcans.

no wonder they pour
their plum-like hearts
into our purple mischief and mayhem
and clap hands at our unhappiness.


but I still don't like the sound
of their laughter.

# I see Hemingway cleaning his shotgun

    I see Virginia Woolf
    loading her pockets
    with river rocks.

```
I see Lorca
on his knees
in the dirt...
he knows exactly
what's about to happen.
```

    I see John Ashbery laughing
    at the Pulitzer Prize committee.

```
I see Kurt Cobain
in the guesthouse
with an idea and a Mossberg,
both borrowed
from Papa.
```

    I see Proust feverishly
    devouring little tea cakes
    when he hits the halfway point
    of writing history's longest novel
    and realizes he's out of ideas.

```
I see Bobbi
who never wrote
—not even a grocery list—
scrawling in cartoonish cursive
loops like skywriting across the blue.
```

I see some of the best writers
never quite getting around
to finishing their book,
and some of the worst
putting out too many.

and I see Confucius and Lao Tzu
smirking at those last two there.

but mostly I see the 19 survivors
of the Brooklyn Bridge leap
every goddamn one sheepishly telling
the same goddamn tale, which went:

"and as soon as I let go,
the minute my feet left the rail,
all I could think was,

*o my god*
*my sweet Jesus*
*I have just*
*made a*
*terrible*
*terrible*
*mistake.*"

## this is not a poem

this is a mouse growling,
gouging out the cat's eye,
and escaping for a change.

this is a trash-tree
that has outgrown all
the trees with names
shooting up through their shadows
and stealing all of their light.

this is the sixth,
     maybe seventh,
          circle of hell.

this is that one cloud
crawling and doodling
in the otherwise blank
and unpunctuated sky.

this is a guitar with strings
strung across the hole
of a scarred mind,
taut and ready.

this is the last
motherfucking cigarette
in the last
motherfucking pack
and what am I
supposed to do NOW?

no... these are words
that just grew tired
of shitty prose

and simply quit
going all the way
to the margin.

# the wrecking ball of dreams

put this on a sign over the doors
to every elementary school...

    where we teach our children
    to fill in empty little circles
    with a Number 2 pencil
    in order to become
    more useful to society,

    and where we feed them patties
    of ammonia-washed animal parts
    with plastic-wrapped honeybuns
    heated up in microwave ovens.

post it at the top of the steps
up to every courthouse...

    where fathers beg for joint custody,
    are sometimes even awarded it,
    then discover over the years
    that there's no fucking
    such thing,

    and where repeat offenders
    come for yet another conviction
    because the powdered eggs and
    moldy mattress with jizz stains
    smell better here on the inside.

hang a big banner with it
writ large, and in red letters,
over every entrance to Congress...

where our elected representatives
wearing scarlet striped ties come
to continue honing their skills
in reaching further
and further
under the table.


and then, last of all,
tattoo it across my back
in large letters
of lampblack ink...

so that when I carry it,
I bear the load weight
where it belongs,
across these dumb broad shoulders
of the one who is at fault.

the elephant dreams with you now

so,
when the sun
burns your eyes,
even around corners
and in the shade...

and the night seems
darker than ever...

and the alarm clock
sounds like it's smothering
all of the things you'd actually
wanted to do with your life...

and the rheumatic ache that festers
between the nubs of your bones
begins before you can even
stumble into the shower,

remember this one
good elephant
in your life.

the elephant dreams with you now

so,
even then
I knew scant chances
were the laces
of my red gloves.

and his voice
telling me that
I had no business hoping
was the bell
signaling feet flat
on the goddamn canvas
on the right side
of the ropes
still.

and while I can't say
that I always won,
I can say that I
never once lost.

and in dreams with
the elephant smiling,
I ride on his back.

## dying for and of life

like that lowball glass
of tequila sitting on the bar
that you know needs to be your last.

like counting the things you love
as they recede.

like falling behind
on getting the right number
of candles into a cardboard box
on the midnight assembly line
with that fat old supervisor
wheezing down your neck
whose wife's at home
doin' the mailman.

like crying on the way to get more
and going anyway.

like the moment you find out it's *you*—
*you* whose attempt at being a dad
caused her sixteen years of stress—
*you* whose wife is at the therapist
crying right now.

like laughing at the
blood in the barrel
when it's not
funny at all.

the sidewalks frighten me

crawling
with Converse low-tops
anxious to make the microbial
front door of a Burger King,

teeming
with the shiny purple
and pink-striped shopping bags
of our descent into levels of hell
we've yet to fully explore,

bobbing
with smartphones and tablets—
the fireflies of imaginary conversations
with ex-girlfriends who miraculously
care again, parents who tried to love us,
and presidents who did not save us,

and wanting
this river of human trash,
the debris of the mammalian diaspora,
to carry me its course
to the unseen sea.

all my critics

best to remember
who's the bull here
and who's the matador
in the blood sport of words.

I can throw up more red capes
in your face than you will ever
care to charge, as I slowly
wear you down to dust
with my footwork
and lances.

the game,
like roulette,
is designed
for you to lose.

anyway...
happy snorting.

and I look forward
to your next
review.

all my critics

has anyone ever
tattooed your reviews
onto their skin so
they never forget?

    I didn't
    think so.

so why don't you
just fuck right off?

# we're fools, of course

it's how most men
make it through life—
    by doing a good deal
    of not thinking about this.

look at Martin Luther,
or... say... Joan of Arc—
    who was, let's be honest,
    more of a man than I—

and we see where being
clinically thoughtful
will get you.

and as fools go,
we're top o' the line—

    few have ignored more
    for as long or more
    thoroughly than we.

like Virtue,
being a fool is
its own reward, I suppose.

only easier,
and far more
enjoyable.

# Schopenhauer laughed for 72 years

knowing
that even after
we'd bought and read
all his big fat books
and dissertations,

we were still
gonna go ahead
and do what we
damn well pleased
anyway.

he would pause between
gales of laughter,
wipe his eyes
and catch his breath,

then continue scratching
pen on paper
pointlessly.

eunuchs are more exact

especially
when it comes
to the measuring
and the magnitude
of all that has been lost.


if you really
want to know
how much a thing
actually costs, then
ask someone who has
already paid.

# every time my toilet flushes

Lake Thunderbird
drops another inch.

someone somewhere thinks
of their grandfather.

"they can hear it,"
says Bukowski.

I wait there a minute or two and then
jiggle the handle.

I feel like I've lost
yet another part of me.

some small voice
I can't stand
says: "What NOW?"

I remember the day
I deposited my dissertation
in the bowels of the library.

it's easier to pretend
there are no consequences.

I think of her
last words to me.

I didn't recite them Shelley

but I thought about it...

to the couple talking on smartphones
to children and grumpy clients
at their table right next to
my $70 dinner last night...

to the stripper who lurched
into the coffee shop this morning
after a rough night at work
that she told us all about
in a smoke-encrusted voice
pitched to a hard volume
that would cut through
a din of hollering
and horny men...

and to Congress during
this week's special session.

I mean, right up to the point
at which the secret service
grabbed me by the scrotum
to help me find my way out.

# I didn't recite them Shelley

but I thought about it...

to the kid behind the counter
of the convenience store
after he suggested a banana
as the perfect snack
—it comes in nature's own packaging—
he said earnestly...

to the Ethiopian housekeeping lady
at the Providence Mo-6... though
I'm sure it would have delighted her,
I fear her English was not up to the
task. but then, who the fuck am I
to say a thing like that...

and to my friend as we burned
the miles like the furniture
of a snowbound shack, taking
comfort which WILL run out.

but I'm not sure we have time
for poetry, much less
that prancer Shelley.

## said the skeleton

don't assume
all the glorious places
you think you're gonna go
and things you believe
you're gonna do in life
are necessarily better
than all the ones
I went and did.

don't forget
that there is
one of me
inside of each
and every one
of you.

remember,
as the planet
burns down around us,
how much cooler it tends
to be a good six feet
under ground.

and that, once
the buttery baby fat
has turned into meat,
then muscle, then softens
and sags and wattles and
finally wastes away,
I'll still be right
here, right in

the center of you, hard
and white, and right,
and remorseless.

    said the skeleton:

        and you think
        life
        is boring?

# use a lot of toilet paper

and set aside plenty
of time for it.

like poetry and sex,
we miss certain things
when we rush it.

remember:
few joys in life
are as pure as these three.


and accept the nature
of the act itself.

like poetry and sex,
vital, unavoidable pursuits
tend to be messy.

## the damnation of Faust

why blame Mephistopheles?

he was only trying to help
with an immediate problem,

    as devils often do.

and souls,
bless their hearts,
have to get from here
to somewhere.


and Faust?
         poor Faust
backed into some dark corner
and bleating:

   "I only meant to..."
     and
   "would that I have..."

you stupid, stupid bastard...

did you think it mattered
whether you shook
the right hand
or the left
to seal your agreement?

men often crawl

the likeness
of my friend, Dora,
replaced the sad portrait
of the pedophile, Sandusky,
on the famous Penn State mural
after those murderous years
he was allowed to torture
teens in the university's
locker rooms and showers.

this, after a man she guesses
she thought she loved came
deathly close to strangling
all the ideas she guesses
she thought she'd had
about their future
right out of her—

by way of her throat pressed
deep into the mattress
of their bed.

and now,
she writes poems
and goes into prisons
to try and convince other
men who crawl
to walk more
upright.

men often crawl

by choice
through the wreckage and
across the broken glass and
sharp stones,

licked by flame and
stung by poisoned smoke
till their palms and knees
begin to bleed a bit.

men often crawl
in order to prepare themselves
for the business
of standing up.

the way a fly lives


    eat.
    shit.
    and die.


don't
forget
the reproducing.

more
eating
shitting
and dying.

# it is somehow enjoyable

to believe with absolute certainty
in concepts that are implausible,
if not outright ridiculous.

   to sit in the morning shadows of the class
   that did not make, a semester's lost wages,
   and sip coffee with toast.

to willfully cruelly delightfully
force people into explaining
what that emoticon they just
used "really means."

   to drive the crusty edges of cotton fields
   and cattle yards where two panhandles meet
   on the way to some half-sold gig in Santa Fe
   that won't make enough for expenses.

that while I didn't get to do
everything I wanted to, I got to do
a lot of things I didn't know
I wanted to.

   to know that I have no choice
   but to die before I retire.

to watch the cats and dogs
without besmirching their actions
by assigning them human motives.

# and nobody stops it

the reality shows
that dissolve reality
on contact.

the selling of dirty tap water
in slightly blue-ish
plastic bottles.

the Burned Man
screaming at the corner
of Normandie and La Posada.

Hollywood's next script
for a romantic comedy
starring Vince Vaughn
and Jennifer Aniston.

the Greeters,
the goddamned
Walmart Greeters.

ESPN's talking heads who over-
use their thesauruses, and words
like "penetration" and "skill set."

the parents
that shouldn't be,
and the children
that can't be.

the Transportation
Security Administration.
or Department of Motor Vehicles.

all the people who think
they know what's best
for all the people.

Rush Limbaugh's
sanctioned rape
of the radio waves.

and the bombs

    and the bombs...

        and the bombs...

## only Hollywood Boulevard

only there,
between a Hard Rock
and the glitzy Kodak Theater,
would I have witnessed a bookie,
with mirrored shades and a black
ponytail whipping back and forth
as he kept an eye on sidewalk traffic,
count out small bills, the piddly gains,
but mostly losses, of a man-sized Elmo
standing—slump-shouldered and oh so
pink, just a filthy and deflated balloon
of fuzzy Muppet with big plastic eyes
wide from worry—there before him.

all that, while a yellow-orange Tigger
of about the same size and shagginess
looked away in shame, wondering how
he would explain this to Pooh and Piglet.

and the bookie did not seem to care,
nor remember his rapturous days
of childhood morning television.

and Elmo looked so full
of polyfoam and regret.

and I stood by, brokenhearted,
defeated by the crime and general
decline of the neighborhood,
here on the streets of Sesame.

only Hollywood Boulevard

I had moved to Hollywood
after the comical collapse of my band,
and we were living in an apartment
building off the boulevard proper.

it was '87 and Hollywood
was a Technicolor Babylon.
the whole place was seething.

my first night there, I went
for a stroll down the boulevard.
    punks, hookers, tourists,
    transvestites, metal-heads,
    and wide-eyed refugees
    from El Salvador, addicts
    and actors and assholes...
    life's rich pageant.

there was a panhandler
using a badly broken and
defaced ventriloquist's dummy
to solicit passers by.
he would shove the horrifying
little mannequin into people's faces
and clack its wooden jaws together
while screaming

    *GIMMEADOLLAR!!! GIMMEADOLLAR!!!*

and I remember thinking to myself:
    *I do believe I can work with this.*

and then I walked into the first
bar I came to.

## as cordial as a bonbon

Jon Dee just told the city
of Des Moines: *Fuck you!*

then shook the dust from his sandals
and headed for South Dakota.

he may not have been wearing sandals,
but he did leave for South Dakota.

```
in the sprawl of bars
and the currents of
bourbon
among the liars and
cowards and
kindness
of spirits...

just because everyone can
doesn't mean
everyone should.

but if you have to,
well then,
that's that.
```

and I say:
*Let's go to
South Dakota.*

poetry won't save us

but neither will one more
teenager with dreadlocks
and dad's $3,000 guitar
in the tiny back seat
of a Toyota Prius.

and neither will one more
episode of "Honey Boo Boo."
not even the Oxygen Network,
nor, let's be honest, PBS.

and I doubt it will be
the right reverend
Sun Myung Moon,
or our man Joel Osteen
and his million-dollar smile
blinging for God up over 610
in Houston's soot and steam.

because here is the blameless,
stainless steel Truth
of Our Condition:

if we are waiting
for somebody or something
to somehow save us,
we die lost.

# Americans don't know

what Americans don't know
would stun even the prophets.
and they're quite accustomed
to the ignorance of nations.

what Americans don't know
is that what goes for the
Amazon Horned Frog
goes for humans as well:
    that no species
    in any ecosystem
    is allowed unchecked growth.

what Americans don't know
is that a common greeting
among certain Sulawesi men
in the mountains of Indonesia
is to gently grab and squeeze
each other's testicles.

what Americans don't know
could float a big-ass boat,
fill the Grand Canyon,
be spread as a condiment
on every bun of every burger
served in every McDonalds for a week
with plenty left over to go around.

old age arrives on schedule

and begins to unpack
in the mothball stench
of its suitcases and bags.

it hangs things, uninvited,
in the back bedroom closet
wanting to make quite clear
it is not going to leave.


old age arrives on schedule

which means 20 minutes
earlier than expected,

allowing extra time
for asking the exact
same question 4 times,

and for the anger,
    for the bafflement,
        for the slipping away.

then we will eat dinner at 5:30.

# I saw Christ in there

in the top drawer
of my desk, where I
keep That Other Thing.

    in the threadbare sound hole
    of that dreadnaught guitar.

in the scar that runs down
the center of my chest
and bisects my navel.

    deep in the black sadness
    of her eyes the last time
    she ever looked at me.

in that tiny holy
gap between breaths
where my *No* becomes *Yes*.

    in the left-hand pocket
    of the stripper's red purse
    when she fished around
    for a stick of Juicy Fruit.

in the dirty fist
of the Crack Queen,
tucked in the folds
of his ragged prom dress,
tangled up in Chore Boy.

and I saw Christ in there,
all huddled up in the corner
of his old garden tomb... saying
he'd given it his best, but now
he's tired after 2,000 years
and just doesn't want
to do it anymore.

## at the airport

where we sit for coffee before we head over
to Gate 18 and begin to question, hard,
the "science" of aerodynamics.

where we note how—
just like a slaughterhouse—
we are funneled into smaller
and straighter lines until
we pass, one by one, down
That Dark Narrow Hallway.

where, at the Beach House
in LAX, Terminal 8, we order
a double shot of the Herradura
for $15 because the single is $12,
and LAX smells like a new hospital,
and because the terminals are named
"terminals" and we've only completed
the first leg of a two-damn-day journey
and we're still not at all convinced
that those so-called "laws"
of aerodynamics
ring true.

where all the women seem
mysterious and their attraction
more profound and irresistible
simply because We Will Likely
Never See Them Again.

and where, in line at Gate 85,
waiting for the next flight,
and a good bit buzzed,
we mumble the words,
just over our breaths,
    "Lift… Weight…
    Thrust… Drag."

# another war is building for another reason

because, really,
the world can't go too long
without one.

because there are stones,
and they must be thrown.

because, otherwise,
people will start twiddling
their index and middle fingers,
then mixing their medications,

and before too long, we'll all be
zoned out in front of a 24-hour
marathon of "Ice Road Truckers"
with broken needles sticking out our necks.

because, you know,
Cain and Abel and all that...
it wasn't land or oil or religion,

they had everything there was to have,
save one thing:
War.

# fact is an artifice

like a house is an edifice,
it was constructed by man.

the devil can't live
in a stone or a tree.
he needs a house.

a fact is man's work,

and the devil's favorite
tool to keep him tuned
to the five o'clock news.


whenever someone says
"look at the facts,"
it's an act of misdirection,

like a cheap magician's
fluttering hand, or

the politician's half-told
lies that help him steal
and seal the election.

# everybody knew it was me

who sold Lindsey Lohan
her first OxyContin.

> when the university's new
> and very expensive library
> burned to the ground.

when the Rolling Brownouts began.
but, my apartment was really
fucking hot that summer.

> who stuck the big cross
> covered in rainbow ribbons,
> pink flags, and donkey buttons
> out in Rush Limbaugh's front yard
> that night after his most racist episode.

that Christ was talking about
with that throwing the first
stone business... I mean,
he was looking
*right at me.*

> whose sad lack of desire
> to ever own anything
> —or to hold down
> any kind of real work
> out in the real world—
> caused the recession.

who stole that Christmas
tree from The Optimist lot.

nobody said it...

but...

the gods are dead

and they will be missed.

life was so much easier when
that dark cloud of certainty
hung over every decision.
every victory.
every defeat.

but alas, as happens with
so many left in charge,
they began to bicker.

and within the span
of only a few millennia,
divisions formed,
which, of course,
led to denominations.

and once that great hammer
strikes its nail...
                    well...
they really had no chance.

the gods are dead

and rest buried
in unmarked graves.

dead of neglect
along with the others,
they are interred in
the endless Potter's Field,
filled with Dead Gods...
too many to count.

new gods are born
each day, filled with
compassion and righteous rage,
and with truth and love
and horror and
incomprehensible
power.

we'll kill them too.

church is over

and it's noon on a Sunday,
unless you go to one of those
with a preacher who hears
a lot more from God...

and the streets flood with white
Escalades and jet-black Lexuses,
their back bumpers proclaiming
to those of us who just got up
that we are all going to hell,
while the front bumpers
ride our sleepy asses...

and all the Applebee's and
El Chico's along the interstate
fill to their gills with the world's
worst fucking tippers, stiffing
college undergrads who are
just trying to buy books...

church is over

before I'm even dressed,
so y'all just go on
and start without me.

most of my weeks I've been
up all night arm-wrestling Satan
and arguing with God anyway, so
by the time morning services
roll around I've pretty much
done all the heavy lifting
and said my piece already.

I can't figure out how
you church folk can squeeze in
everything that needs to be said
and sworn and done and undone
in less than two hours
on a Sunday morning.

and last time I went,
it mainly seemed to be
a bunch of uncomfortable people
wearing uncomfortable clothes
sitting on uncomfortable benches
sweating out an uncomfortable silence.

I had just about decided
that the silence was
the best part, but
by then Church
was over.

# look up from the Bible

look up from the Bible.
God—as most authors
often are—is probably
somewhat embarrassed
by his earlier works.

look up from the Bible
and imagine that everyone
you see is your 'neighbor'
and then... remember what
it says to do about that.

it'll be hard, but, hey,
it's not a buffet where
you pick and choose.

look up from the Bible
to a torched and sotted
world in desperate need
of a Newer Testament.

look up from the Bible
and then count to ten,
and then look back down
and see that all it is,
see, is a BOOK.

look up from the Bible.
the ossified prophets
want you to look them
in the bloodshot eye.

look up from the Bible,
written in a dead language,
then translated into another
dead language, then compiled,
edited, rewritten, added to,
and redacted by over a thousand
dead men... then tell me again
it's The Sacred Word of God.

# the burgermeister of that town

he pretty much
runs the place,

and I've always been
happy for him to do it.

citizens are a general
pain in the municipal ass.

and it's not an elected
position, per se.

he thinks well of himself and wears
a hat with a big feather on it.

you could wax a sled
with his shiny mustachio.

but, goodchrist, *someone*
has to take care of things, right?

I've heard his son has ambition,
but also has a Filipino wife.

the citizens suspect
he is always scheming,

but he knows for *sure*
the citizens *are* a general
pain in the municipal ass.

# 22 cans of Campbell's soup

is 22 days of not
necessarily
having to go
to the grocery store.

is a good start on
3 or 4 Warhol Tributes.

is 11 sets
of tin-can telephones
connected by 11 strands
of cotton string.

is 9 whys,
7 why nots
and 6 why bothers.

is 17,600 milligrams
of sodium.

and will require
6 gallons of water
(or milk, for creamed soups)
eventually.

## in the middle of Texas

the hell-hearted sun,
in the middle of August,
can drive its golden nail
straight through the planet
and out the other side,

until all those Chinamen
can tell you just how hot
it really is—
Hell-off-its-hinges hot.

in the middle of Texas
the scorpions, fire ants,
and fiddleback spiders are
winning the real estate war,

and have been since before
the Bering land-bridge went under,

when the first Comanche pitched
his first lodge-pole in Texas and
had to brush away the ancient biters.

(anyone who thinks they have dominion
over Texas is a goddamn fool.)

in the middle of Texas
we shoot first,
and don't bother
to ask questions later,

unless the questions are:

    "you got any more?"

or

    "help me drag'em up onto the porch?"

# I live without working

I knew
from the time
I first saw the original
"Raiders of the Lost Ark,"
back in '83, that I would never

sit behind a some-assembly-required
particle-board desk under buzzing
fluorescent lights in some glaring,
linoleum-tiled prairie dog village,
making cold calls for the man.

and though I love poetry,
I can't say it's a living.

and it does require
a lot more work
than I care for.

so, thinking about it
now, I guess I should've
gone with archeology.

# I live without working

or at least that's what
some Jackass said
about what I do.

he may or may not be stupid,
but he is certainly ignorant.

TO LIVE IS TO WORK.
   ask the ants
   ask the salmon
   ask the swift
   ask my Uncle Tinker...

or ask poor old Homeless Job
pushing his shopping cart
full of junk that he imagines
he might sell and sometimes does
(but it's rare to find someone
drunk enough to buy an 8-track tape).

ask the millions of extinct species
and the millions of blood-lines
stopped dead in their tracks
because they were unequal to
the job of the work of living.
Jackass.

let's call this fiction

since I never promised
otherwise.

since I'd rather not
do 5 to 10 for something
that only kind of happened
anyway.

since that particular woman
would sue the blue jeans
right off my ass
if I told the facts.


let's call this fiction

    said the birds
       to the bees...

    said the writer
       to his agent...

    said the gods
       to their prophets.

let's call this fiction

although I can
safely say that
it's certainly more
True than what
actually did occur.

since words like
"fact" & "fiction"
"true" & "false"
"did" & "didn't"
are approximate
at their best.

since you were
not even there
and so... how
could you know
either way? so...
why bother yourself?

# the last number on the program

since the Bay City Rollers
were taken by Liam Neeson
in that movie where, I admit,
he took them well, my fallback
will have to be Luciano Pavarotti
singing that big one from Puccini
in a language I should have learned.

right after a friend stands and says
that Nathan's dying wish was
to have all his poems read
in alphabetical order here
at his funeral, beginning with
the indefinite article 'A'.

and that would be the cue,
since I was only kidding,
for the soundman to click on
the mp3—or whatever the hell
they're using by that time—
        (since Luciano's dead too, so,
        won't be able to sing in person)
as my friend invites all those present
to close their bloodshot eyes
and bow their hung-over heads
before a greatness that few achieve,
and do their best to take in the words
that they too will likely not understand:

*nessun dorma…*        *nessun dorma…*

# the last number on the program

when I die,
here's what I'd like:

a girl piper in the doorway
in full highland drag,
sporting the Graham tartan
(grey-on-grey plaid. surprised?)
to pipe *Amazing Grace*,

as one friend
after another
tells the most
outrageous
funny
shameful
heartbreaking
triumphant
humiliating
True Stories
of who I was and what I did.

and there should be an open bar
just to fuck with all
my sober friends.

we will hardly be able
to pay the piper, but
the open bar will be
very affordable.

right now my tax money


is polishing an expensive
pair of crocodile shoes
in Reagan National Airport
while they wait to catch
a first-class seat
to Palm Springs.


is stiffing a waitress
at the Capital Grille
on Pennsylvania Avenue
because the Pan Seared
Chilean Sea Bass with
Citrus and Pea Tendrils
arrived a few minutes late
and was not as delicate
and buttery as expected.


is hiring the best
asshole-in-a-box
divorce attorney
on the Beltway,
because a bit too much
has been goin' on
in the bathrooms
and all the broom closets
of The House of Representatives.

right now my tax money

is buying 1/324,597$^{th}$
of the ink used to print
the IRS break-room rules.


is sitting somewhere scared
and alone, feeling inferior
to those strapping stacks
of cash from the successful.


is purchasing one-quarter
of a teaspoon of propellant
for a drone-mounted
Hellfire Missile,
which may or may not kill
someone who may or may not
be a terrorist,
or perhaps a bride.

# like the last words of a man in an electric chair

it's that point on the horizon
of every soul where
the bullshit stops,

and it's my father
ripping out the IVs
and his breathing tube
in order to crawl
from his hospital bed
and "close the goddamn gate."

or it's the One-Armed Poet deciding,
in that last year before the cancer
pulled him under its chemo waves,
that he did not have the time
to waste on cheaper tequila
and the good scriptural advice
of old church friends anymore,

and it's the two-fister
sitting on an unmade motel bed
thinking, *goodchrist... apparently*
*enough is NOT enough.*

or it's Goethe asking for
more light,

and it's Hank muttering
into his grey beard,

"Don't try.
Don't even try."


    or it's God thinking,
    "time to pull the big plug
    and let nature take its course,"

and it's Shaitan The Resister
scratching his hot horned head
and wondering out loud
"could I have possibly gotten
all this so very, very wrong?"


    or it's the sun shooting
    its rays across the ocean
    and up onto the shore
    of the quiet morning
               after the apocalypse.

# enough light to know

that given half a chance
I will choose poorly
as often as not.

enough light to know
that it's either early morning
or early evening, and that
either one is okay.

enough light to know
that mom and dad were right
about my first motorcycle,
and my first wife.

enough light to know
that there should be
less light in this bar.

enough light to know
her shape in the bed.

and that's enough light.

# even death will have exits

there are ways out
of the way out,

   and, as I am always
   the night's opening act,
   I'm adept at finding them—

   though, I can't imagine
   what might lie beyond
   the back door of hell.


and even if
the final stage door
opens onto the fiery pit,
the best exit is
only as good as
the best entrance—

like birth, raise
the panic, raise
the chaos, raise
our voices together.


   so... everybody...

      all together now...

         scream *Fire!*

... by the Salton Sea

~ Rodney Bursiel

a few rules for the starving artist
that are really more just guidelines


1) Eat well. Eat large. But eat well and large for
free every chance you get.

2) Never pay for parking. The space may be a
mile from the margaritas you seek. But it exists,
and the walk will do you some amount of good.
Before, and after, you drink them.

3) Learn to love and appreciate the worn contours
and mushy concavity of the big couches of decent
strangers who support the arts. But sleep with at
least one eye half open.

4) Drive someone, anyone, else's car to out-of-
town gigs whenever possible. I will not loan you
mine, though. Even if I ever start to make any
money at this god-forsaken art and actually buy
one someday.

5) Tip your waitresses, waiters, and especially your
bartenders. And tip them well. They are all you've
got on the road. And their jobs suck just as much
fiscal ass as yours.

6) One truly good guitar will serve you better than
20 flashy ones that winked at you once from the
window of some music store. Okay. Maybe two.

7) Therapy is not a dirty word. And those who joke or give you shit about it need it more than you do. Some of our best jumped from bridges, cut their own ears off, and filled their coat pockets with big river stones for lack of the good counsel of a good soul who truly knows what she is doing.

a few rules for the starving artist
that are really more just guidelines

1) Be certain you are an artist. Sure,
you're starving. Maybe it's because
you're lazy. Or untalented. It could
be a lot of things, really.

2) Please understand: Words are under
no obligation to you. Just because you
expect them to accomplish this or that
doesn't mean they will. Words don't
give a single damn about you or what
you want. Can you be okay with that?
Think before answering.

3) Being profoundly unhappy does not
add depth or substance, it only
worries your family and exasperates
your friends. Angst is for amateurs.
Sylvia Plath wrote *in spite* of her
depression not *because of* her
depression.

4) Are you even listening? These are
unimportant. Quit staring out the
window like that. It's creepy.

5) Is writing well what you want with
every atom of every molecule of every
ounce of everything you are? WOW. Then
I really hope it works out for you.

6) Don't be clever. It's a college-
boy's crutch.

7) Don't be deliberately obscure.
Because there is a weather vane that
spins a yarn in the feathered east...
listen... you are NOT Cormac
McCarthy... you will need to use a
semi-colon or question mark now and
then.

**Nathan Brown** is an author, songwriter, and award-winning poet living in Wimberley, Texas. He holds a PhD in English and Journalism from the University of Oklahoma where he taught for seventeen years. And he served as Poet Laureate for the State of Oklahoma in 2013/14.

He has published twelve previous books. *Karma Crisis: New and Selected Poems* was a finalist for the *Paterson Poetry Prize* and the *Oklahoma Book Award*. And his earlier book, *Two Tables Over*, won the *2009 Oklahoma Book Award*.

He travels too much, offering concerts, readings, and workshops, and would prefer to stay home and dry-stack stones all over his property, much to the bother and concern of his neighbors.

Naomi Shihab Nye recently said about Nathan: "… a tilted long-ranging eye that sees the next bend in the road even when he's standing right here, firmly planted."

*

**Jon Dee Graham** is a musician, guitarist, and songwriter from Austin, Texas. He was named Austin Musician of the Year during the South by Southwest music conference in 2006 and is the only artist to

be inducted into the Austin Music
Hall of Fame three times: as a solo
artist in 2000, again in 2008 as a
member of The Skunks, and again in
2009 as a member of the True
Believers.

The Skunks were pioneers in the
Texas punk rock scene, sharing
bills with John Cale, The Ramones,
and The Clash.

The True Believers, which included
Alejandro Escovedo and his brother,
Javier Escovedo, are widely
considered by critics to be seminal
figures in the fusion of literary
songwriting and punk rock, as well
as being in the vanguard of
blending country, blues, and pure
adrenal rock into a genre known
variously as "alt country,"
"roots," or "No Depression."

Graham lives with his wife,
Gretchen (AKA 'The Professor') and
their son William in Austin, TX,
and tours more or less constantly.

In his downtime, he draws bears.

CPSIA information can be obtained
at www.ICGtesting.com
Printed in the USA
FSOW02n1231080117
29257FS

9 780983 738374